Romantic Questions

Gregory J.P. Godek

bestselling author of *1001 Ways to Be Romantic*

CASABLANCA PRESS
A DIVISION OF SOURCEBOOKS
NAPERVILLE, IL

Published by: Sourcebooks, Inc.
P.O. Box 372, Naperville, Illinois 60566
(630) 961-3900
FAX: (630) 961-2168

Cover design by Scott Theisen
Internal design and production by Andrew Sardina, Scott Theisen
and Joe Leamon

𝒟edication

*To everyone who questions. To lovers who seek the depths of their
relationships. To everyone who questions the status quo. And to the
childlike quality in you that questions everything.*

*And, of course, to my Bride, Tracey—who answered "Yes!" when I
asked her the most important question I've ever asked anyone.*

Library of Congress Cataloging-in-Publication Data
Godek, Gregory J.P.
         Romantic questions / by Gregory J.P. Godek
              p.   cm. — (A Casablanca book)
         ISBN 1-57071-152-6 (pbk.)
         1. Man-woman relationships — Miscellanea.   2. Intimacy
(Psychology) — Miscellanea.   3. Love — Miscellanea.   I. Title.   II. Series.
HQ801.G565   1997
306.7 — dc21   96-50431
                                                                      CIP

Printed and bound in the United States of America.

10 9 8 7 6 5 4 3 2 1

Contents

Introduction

$\mathscr{A}$ book of questions should begin with questions, don't you think?

Why did you buy this book? What do you hope to discover about yourself? What do you hope to learn about your partner? Are you seeking a method for exploring yourself and your relationship? If so, this book is designed specifically as a tool to help you on your path of discovery.

Questions are powerful. Questions are tools. Questions can be points of leverage. Questions can challenge your assumptions and beliefs. Questions lead to answers!

Some of the questions in this book are deceptively simple. Some are familiar—but deserve revisiting. Some may be shocking. But all of them are designed to help you understand yourself, your partner and your relationship.

So, why don't we get started??

Gregory J. P. Godek
January 1997

Partnership

We partner up, two-by-two, automatically.
Human beings seem to function better in pairs.
This does NOT mean, however, that it's going to be easy!

1

☐ Me
☐ My Partner

*W*hat are the three best things about your partner?

2

☐ Me
☐ My Partner

*W*hat made you fall in love with your partner?

3

☐ Me
☐ My Partner

*W*hat do you and your partner usually argue about?

A Question of Balance

*Successful couples are good at balancing their needs,
wants and different personalities.*

1

☐ Me
☐ My Partner

*H*ow do you balance your needs
with your partner's needs?

2

☐ Me
☐ My Partner

*H*ow do you balance the needs
of your relationship with each of your
individual needs?

3

☐ Me
☐ My Partner

*H*ow do you balance family and
friends? Kids and spouse? Yourself
and your partner?

4

☐ Me
☐ My Partner

*H*ow do you balance work
and play? Your strengths and
weaknesses?

5

❑ Me
❑ My Partner

*H*ow do you balance the realities of your life today with your dreams and visions?

6

❑ Me
❑ My Partner

*H*ow do you balance your personal life, professional life and social life?

7

❑ Me
❑ My Partner

*H*ow do you balance your emotional, physical and spiritual needs?

8

❑ Me
❑ My Partner

*H*ow do you balance your short-term needs and your long-term goals?

9

❑ Me
❑ My Partner

*J*ust how important is balance, anyway?

Battle of the Sexes

Last I checked, men and women weren't at war.
Let's declare "peace" in the Battle of the Sexes, okay?

1

☐ Me
☐ My Partner

*W*hat is the most mysterious thing about the opposite sex?

2

☐ Me
☐ My Partner

*W*hat's wrong with men? What's wrong with women?

3

☐ Me
☐ My Partner

*H*ave you ever been infatuated? Describe the feeling. Describe the relationship.

4

☐ Me
☐ My Partner

*D*o you consider yourself/your attitudes/your beliefs to be fairly typical for your gender?

5

☐ Me
☐ My Partner

*W*hat is the one thing that the opposite gender simply doesn't "get" about your gender?

6

☐ Me
☐ My Partner

*W*hat could members of the opposite sex learn by listening to you?

7

☐ Me
☐ My Partner

*I*f you were going to write a self-help relationship book, what would you title it?

8

☐ Me
☐ My Partner

*A*re there any circumstances in which it would be appropriate for a man to physically strike a woman?

9
. . .

☐ Me
☐ My Partner

*W*hat was your most embarrassing moment in the presence of a member of the opposite sex?

Beliefs

How your life unfolds is largely the result of the things you believe. (Do you believe this?)

1
. . .

☐ Me
☐ My Partner

*D*o you believe in love at first sight?

2
. . .

☐ Me
☐ My Partner

*D*o you believe in karma?

3
. . .

☐ Me
☐ My Partner

*D*o you believe in an afterlife? In heaven? In hell? Reincarnation?

4

□ Me
□ My Partner

*D*o you believe in astrology?
Tarot? Palmistry?

5

□ Me
□ My Partner

*D*o you believe in the religion you
were raised in?

6

□ Me
□ My Partner

*D*o you believe that two people
can be "Soul Mates"?

7

□ Me
□ My Partner

*D*o you believe that the Bible is
the inspired Word of God? Do you
believe it literally—or do you believe
it's open to interpretation?

8

□ Me
□ My Partner

*D*o you believe it's proper for
people to express their feelings in
public?

9

❑ Me
❑ My Partner

$\mathcal{D}$o you believe that people learn from their mistakes?

10

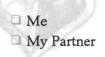

❑ Me
❑ My Partner

$\mathcal{D}$o you believe that blondes have more fun?

11

❑ Me
❑ My Partner

$\mathcal{D}$o you believe in the "American Dream"? (What is the "American Dream"?)

Business as Usual

What is your "world view"? How do your views coincide and differ from those of your partner?

1

❑ Me
❑ My Partner

$\mathcal{D}$o you believe that most politicians are dishonest?

2

☐ Me
☐ My Partner

*D*o you believe that most people are honest?

3

☐ Me
☐ My Partner

*S*hould smoking tobacco be banned? Should smoking marijuana be legalized?

4

☐ Me
☐ My Partner

*S*hould handguns be licensed? Should toy guns be banned?

5

☐ Me
☐ My Partner

*W*hat's the biggest mistake your boss has made lately? If you were in charge, what changes would you make?

What If . . .

*What if...you were to suspend your critical mind
and cynicism—and just "let yourself go"?!*

1

☐ Me
☐ My Partner

*W*hat if you had to tell the
absolute truth for one solid week?

2

☐ Me
☐ My Partner

*W*hat if you could be a comic
strip character...Who would you be?

3

☐ Me
☐ My Partner

*W*hat if blue smoke came out of
your ears every time you became sexually aroused the least little bit?

4

☐ Me
☐ My Partner

*W*hat if you could create the
absolute, perfect job for yourself...
What would it be?

Change

You will experience lots of change in any long-term relationship.
Don't let it take you by surprise!

1
. . .

☐ Me
☐ My Partner

*H*ow does change happen in your life? Are there any patterns that may be significant?

2
. . .

☐ Me
☐ My Partner

*I*s change sudden and dramatic? Or does it happen slowly, more like an evolutionary process?

3
. . .

☐ Me
☐ My Partner

*W*hat kind of change do you face most calmly? What kind of change is most emotional for you?

4

☐ Me
☐ My Partner

*H*ow have you changed for the better? How have you changed for the worse?

5

☐ Me
☐ My Partner

*D*o you change? Or do things change around you?

6

☐ Me
☐ My Partner

*W*hat was the single most significant turning point in your life?

7

☐ Me
☐ My Partner

*W*hat person has helped you change for the better?

8

☐ Me
☐ My Partner

*W*hat book, movie, song, play, etc., has helped you change for the better?

9

☐ Me
☐ My Partner

*H*ow do you handle unpredictable situations?

10

☐ Me
☐ My Partner

*H*ow do you think your life will change most dramatically in the next five years? Ten years? Twenty years?

Clarifications

It helps if the two of you are "talking the same language." There's no absolute "right" and "wrong"—so let's clarify a few terms.

1

☐ Me
☐ My Partner

*W*hat's the difference between love, romance and sex?

2

☐ Me
☐ My Partner

*W*hat's the difference between sexuality and sensuality?

3
· · ·

☐ Me
☐ My Partner

*W*hat's the difference between having sex and making love?

Wishes

Wishing on a star is a good first step—it clarifies your dreams and desires. The second step is to crystalize those dreams into realistic goals.

1
· · ·

☐ Me
☐ My Partner

*I*f you had three wishes, what would they be? (And no, you cannot wish for an infinite number of wishes! Don't be greedy.)

2
· · ·

☐ Me
☐ My Partner

*Y*ou can instantly become a virtuoso musician on one instrument. What instrument is it?

3

☐ Me
☐ My Partner

You've suddenly become the most eloquent, talented public speaker of this generation... and you're about to address a crowd of 50,000 in Yankee Stadium. What is the message you're going to deliver?

4

☐ Me
☐ My Partner

What do you wish for your children?

Could You...?

Do you know what your capabilities are? It's wise to know your limitations; it's exhilarating to push your limits.

1

☐ Me
☐ My Partner

Could you run five miles right now?

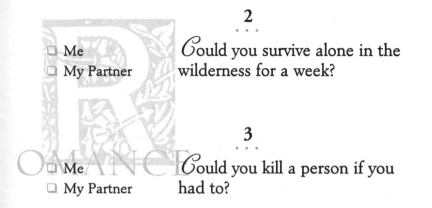

2

☐ Me
☐ My Partner

*C*ould you survive alone in the wilderness for a week?

3

☐ Me
☐ My Partner

*C*ould you kill a person if you had to?

4

☐ Me
☐ My Partner

*C*ould you live for a year in a tent with your partner? (Without going crazy?!)

5

☐ Me
☐ My Partner

*C*ould you change jobs and move to a different city to be with your mate?

Do You...?

Your beliefs are a key to your personality. They affect your everyday behavior and how you treat your partner.

1

☐ Me
☐ My Partner

*D*o you expect that things will generally turn out for the best?

2

☐ Me
☐ My Partner

*D*o you vote?

3

☐ Me
☐ My Partner

*D*o you believe in God?

4

☐ Me
☐ My Partner

*D*o you take good enough care of yourself?

5
. . .

☐ Me
☐ My Partner

*D*o you often re-think your decisions? Or are you always certain that you're right?

Do You Agree?

What is your "Philosophy of Life"? One way of getting a handle on it is to see if you agree or disagree with the following statements:

1
. . .

☐ Me
☐ My Partner

*A*bsence makes the heart grow fonder.

2
. . .

☐ Me
☐ My Partner

*M*oney makes the world go round.

3
. . .

☐ Me
☐ My Partner

*I*t's not whether you win or lose, it's how you play the game.

4

☐ Me
☐ My Partner

All you need is love.

5

☐ Me
☐ My Partner

It is better to give than to receive.

6

☐ Me
☐ My Partner

You reap what you sow.

Dreams

Some people have big dreams. Others just dream their lives away.
How do you deal with your dreams?

1

☐ Me
☐ My Partner

What's your favorite daydream?
(Sexual fantasies don't count for this
question!)

2

❏ Me
❏ My Partner

*W*hat's your dream job? What company? What role? What industry? What product or service?

3

❏ Me
❏ My Partner

*W*hat's your dream home? Where? Why?

4

❏ Me
❏ My Partner

*W*hat is your dream vacation? Where? How long? What activities?

Either-Or

Either, or; this or that; now or then. There's no right or wrong (or is there??)—just your opinion. Either way, your partner deserves to knows more about you!

1

❏ Me
❏ My Partner

*A*re you a peace-keeper or a trouble-maker?

2

☐ Me
☐ My Partner

*A*re you a cat-person or a dog-person?

3

☐ Me
☐ My Partner

*A*re you outspoken or quiet?

4

☐ Me
☐ My Partner

*A*re you humble or arrogant?

5

☐ Me
☐ My Partner

*A*re you an outdoors person or a homebody?

6

☐ Me
☐ My Partner

*A*re you open or secretive?

Erotic

Sure, it's difficult talking about these
intimate issues, but let's give it a try...

1

☐ Me
☐ My Partner

*W*hat's the difference between sexy and erotic?

2

☐ Me
☐ My Partner

*W*hat's the most erotic movie scene you've ever seen?

3

☐ Me
☐ My Partner

*W*hat words do you want to hear during lovemaking?

4

☐ Me
☐ My Partner

*W*hat are the two most sensitive areas of your body?

5

☐ Me

☐ My Partner

*H*ow would you like your partner to dress during lovemaking?

Fame

This is not the time to be modest. Do you feel comfortable sharing your secret desires with your partner?

1

☐ Me

☐ My Partner

*Y*ou're going to be written-up in Who's Who. What will you be famous for?

2

☐ Me

☐ My Partner

*I*f you could accomplish one crazy stunt that would land you in the Guinness Book of World Records, what would it be?

3
. . .

☐ Me
☐ My Partner

If your name were to appear in the dictionary, how would you define yourself?

4
. . .

☐ Me
☐ My Partner

The editors of Bartlett's Familiar Quotations want to include the quote that you're most famous for. What is it?

Family Ties

A great deal of your personality was formed by your family.
So let's take a closer look...

1
. . .

☐ Me
☐ My Partner

How are you just like your father? Your mother?

2

☐ Me
☐ My Partner

*D*o you like the town you grew up in? Describe it.

3

☐ Me
☐ My Partner

*W*hat is your fondest memory from childhood?

4

☐ Me
☐ My Partner

*W*hat is your worst memory from childhood?

5

☐ Me
☐ My Partner

*W*hat were you like as a teenager?

6

☐ Me
☐ My Partner

*W*hen's the last time you called your Mom, just to tell her you love her? Your Dad?

Favorite Things

The better you know your partner, the better you'll be able to find, buy or create appropriate gifts.

1

☐ Me
☐ My Partner

*W*hat is your favorite color?

2

☐ Me
☐ My Partner

*W*hat is your favorite number?

3

☐ Me
☐ My Partner

*W*hat is your favorite movie? Actor? Actress? Comedy? Drama?

4

☐ Me
☐ My Partner

*W*hat is your favorite dinner? Snack food? Fancy restaurant? Fast food restaurant? Dessert?

5

☐ Me
☐ My Partner

*W*hat is your favorite comic strip? Comic character? TV cartoon?

Would You...?

Would you take the time to answer a few questions for your lover?

1

☐ Me
☐ My Partner

*W*ould you ever go skinny-dipping? With your partner in private? With a group of other people?

2

☐ Me
☐ My Partner

*W*ould you pick up a hitchhiker?

3

☐ Me
☐ My Partner

*W*ould you ever run for a political office?

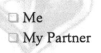

4

☐ Me
☐ My Partner

*W*ould you give money to a homeless person?

5

☐ Me
☐ My Partner

*I*f you were being mugged, would you fight, run or just give them your wallet?

Feelings

Okay, let's get down to it. Let's try some creative ways of expressing our feelings.

1

☐ Me
☐ My Partner

*W*hat movie or TV scene last brought tears to your eyes?

2

☐ Me
☐ My Partner

*W*hat feeling do you have the most difficulty controlling?

3

☐ Me
☐ My Partner

What feeling do you have the most difficulty expressing?

4

☐ Me
☐ My Partner

When is the last time you wrote a love letter?

5

☐ Me
☐ My Partner

What makes you feel most vulnerable?

6

☐ Me
☐ My Partner

When do you feel most fully engaged in living?

7

☐ Me
☐ My Partner

What do you do when you feel blue?

8

☐ Me
☐ My Partner

*W*hat makes you sad? Depressed?

9

☐ Me
☐ My Partner

*W*hat makes you ecstatic? Joyful?

10

☐ Me
☐ My Partner

*W*hen do you feel quietly at peace?

11

☐ Me
☐ My Partner

*W*hat feelings were your parents most uncomfortable expressing? How has this affected you?

12

☐ Me
☐ My Partner

*H*ow do you feel at midnight on New Year's Eve? Christmas morning? Your birthday?

Food, Glorious Food

Is the way to his heart through his stomach? It's worth a try!
(This seems to work equally well for the women—take note, guys.)

1

❑ Me
❑ My Partner

*W*hat is the Best Food In
The World?

2

❑ Me
❑ My Partner

*W*hen you sit down in front of a
great movie, what junk food do you
want within arm's reach?

3

❑ Me
❑ My Partner

*Y*ou can obliterate one kind of food
from the face of the earth. What
food is it?

4

❑ Me
❑ My Partner

*A*re you a picky eater?

5

☐ Me
☐ My Partner

*W*hat is your favorite meal of the day: breakfast, lunch or dinner? Or snacks?!

For Marrieds Only

To have and to hold, for better or for worse, from this day forward, I now pronounce you husband and wife.

1

☐ Me
☐ My Partner

*B*efore anything was "official," how did you know you were going to marry each other?

2

☐ Me
☐ My Partner

*W*here were you when you proposed (or were proposed to)? Exactly what was said?

3

☐ Me
☐ My Partner

*A*s you were growing up, what kind of person did you imagine you'd marry?

4

☐ Me
☐ My Partner

*W*hat is the funniest/most embarrassing/most touching thing that happened during your wedding?

5

☐ Me
☐ My Partner

*D*o you believe that you and your spouse were destined to be together?

For Marrieds Only, Part II

The happiest married couples are those who don't take each other for granted—those who cherish each other in words and action.

1

☐ Me
☐ My Partner

*H*ow do you plan to celebrate your 50th wedding anniversary?

2
. . .

☐ Me
☐ My Partner

*W*hat are your goals as a couple?
How are your goals for yourself supported by your marriage?

3
. . .

☐ Me
☐ My Partner

*D*o you want any (more) children?

4
. . .

☐ Me
☐ My Partner

*S*hould husband and wife be each other's best friend?

For Men Only

Okay, guys, listen up! I know you sometimes have difficulty expressing your feelings. But we all know they're in there...

1
. . .

☐ Me
☐ My Partner

*W*hat's the best thing about being male?

2

□ Me
□ My Partner

*W*hat's the worst thing about being male?

3

□ Me
□ My Partner

*D*o you feel misunderstood by women?

4

□ Me
□ My Partner

*W*hat is your least masculine attribute? Are you uncomfortable talking about it?

5

□ Me
□ My Partner

*W*hich are you more afraid of: cancer or impotence?

6

□ Me
□ My Partner

*I*deally, how often would you like to have sex?

For Singles Only

*Dating shouldn't be about impressing the other person,
but rather about getting him or her to know you better.*

1

☐ Me
☐ My Partner

*C*an you list 25 qualities of your perfect partner?

2

☐ Me
☐ My Partner

*H*ow old do you expect to be when you get married?

3

☐ Me
☐ My Partner

*A*ssuming you won't find a partner who is 100% perfect, what specific characteristics must your partner possess, and which could you live without?

4

☐ Me
☐ My Partner

*H*ow important is it that the person you marry share your religious beliefs?

☐ Me
☐ My Partner

*D*o you want to have children?
How many? Boys or girls? When?

For Singles Only, Part II

*There are no longer "Rules" for dating. The bad news is that
this creates a lot of confusion. The good news is that you're
free to be creative and express yourself.*

1
. . .

☐ Me
☐ My Partner

*W*hat is the best thing about
being single?

2
. . .

☐ Me
☐ My Partner

*W*hat's the worst thing about
being single?

3
. . .

☐ Me
☐ My Partner

*W*hat aspect of the single life
would you like to carry over into your
married life?

4
• • •

☐ Me
☐ My Partner

*W*hat is the minimum length of time two people should date before getting engaged?

5
• • •

☐ Me
☐ My Partner

*H*ow do your life values compare with your partner's? How do your sexual values compare?

For Women Only

Do you think that women are the "fairer sex"?
What do you really want men to understand about women?

1
• • •

☐ Me
☐ My Partner

*W*hat is the best thing about being a woman?

2
• • •

☐ Me
☐ My Partner

*W*hat is the worst thing about being a woman?

3
. . .

☐ Me
☐ My Partner

*D*o you experience PMS? How do you want to be treated during your period?

4
. . .

☐ Me
☐ My Partner

*W*hat is your most masculine trait? Do you use it, or do you tend to suppress it?

5
. . .

☐ Me
☐ My Partner

*D*o you feel misunderstood by men?

6
. . .

☐ Me
☐ My Partner

*A*re you a feminist?

Discover your lover

Fun & Games

Getting in touch with your "inner child" is one thing, but getting him or her to come out and play is another!

1

☐ Me
☐ My Partner

*W*hat was your favorite game as a child?

2

☐ Me
☐ My Partner

*W*hat is your favorite game now?

3

☐ Me
☐ My Partner

*D*o you like crossword puzzles? Jigsaw puzzles? Brainteasers?

4

☐ Me
☐ My Partner

*W*hat would you like to learn to do? (Play guitar? Sail? Learn a new language? Meditate?)

Getting Down to Business

You'll spend a third to half of your waking hours at work.
What are your attitudes toward work? How will your work
habits affect your relationship?

1

☐ Me
☐ My Partner

*D*o you earn what you're worth?

2

☐ Me
☐ My Partner

*D*o top corporate executives earn too much money?

3

☐ Me
☐ My Partner

*S*hould lobbying in Congress be outlawed?

4

☐ Me
☐ My Partner

*A*re there too many lawyers?

❑ Me   *D*o doctors earn too much money?
❑ My Partner   Government workers? Union
                                 members? Teachers?

Getting to Know You

Deep down we all want the same thing:
to be known, understood and appreciated.

1
· · ·

❑ Me   *W*hat three nouns best describe
❑ My Partner   you? Three adjectives?

2
· · ·

❑ Me   *W*hich period of your life did
❑ My Partner   you enjoy the most? Childhood?
                                 Adolescence? Young adulthood?
                                 Adulthood? Right now?

3
. . .

☐ Me
☐ My Partner

*W*hat do you want to be remembered for?

4
. . .

☐ Me
☐ My Partner

*W*ho are you? (How do you define yourself?)

Gilligan's Island

Some of these "crazy" questions can reveal important insights into your personality, values and dreams.

If you were stranded on a desert island...

1
. . .

☐ Me
☐ My Partner

*W*hat food would you miss the most?

2
. . .

☐ Me
☐ My Partner

*W*hat three music albums/CDs would you most like to have?

3

☐ Me
☐ My Partner

*W*ould you wear clothes?

4

☐ Me
☐ My Partner

*W*hat three books would you take along?

5

☐ Me
☐ My Partner

*W*hat one person would you want to be there with you?

Ha-ha-ha-ha-ha!

People in happy long-term relationships know that when all else fails, their sense of humor sees them through.

1

☐ Me
☐ My Partner

*W*hat's your favorite joke?

2

❏ Me
❏ My Partner

*W*hat's the funniest thing you've ever said?

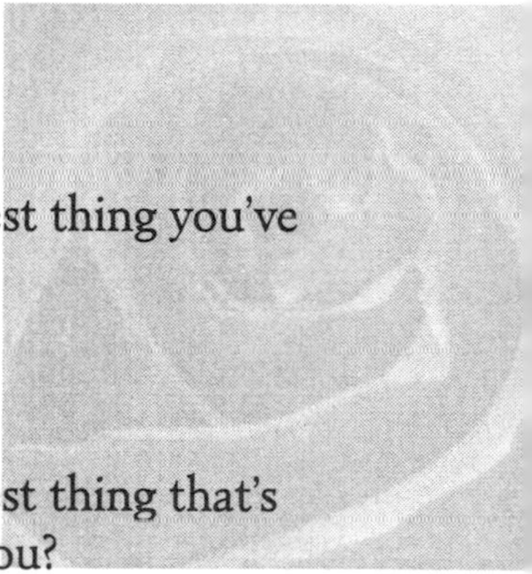

3

❏ Me
❏ My Partner

*W*hat's the funniest thing you've ever done?

4

❏ Me
❏ My Partner

*W*hat's the funniest thing that's ever happened to you?

5

❏ Me
❏ My Partner

*W*hat's the best practical joke you've ever pulled?

6

❏ Me
❏ My Partner

*W*hen have you been doubled over with laughter?

History

Here are some exercises in creative fantasy. Playing the question game of "What if..." can be quite insightful.

1
. . .

☐ Me
☐ My Partner

*I*f you could become one historical figure, who would it be? Would you change anything about the way he or she lived his or her life?

2
. . .

☐ Me
☐ My Partner

*W*hat are the five greatest achievements of humankind?

3
. . .

☐ Me
☐ My Partner

*I*f you could have stopped one war from occurring, which one would it be? Why?

4

☐ Me
☐ My Partner

*Y*ou can go back and participate in the writing of the U.S. Constitution. You can add one new item to the Bill of Rights. What is it?

Hmmm?

How often do you take time to ponder what makes you tick? Curiosity about yourself—and your partner—is a characteristic of life-long lovers.

1

☐ Me
☐ My Partner

*W*hat makes you jealous?

2

☐ Me
☐ My Partner

*W*hat makes you angry?

3

☐ Me
☐ My Partner

*W*hat makes you sad?

4

☐ Me
☐ My Partner

*D*id you read *Bridges of Madison County*? Did Francesca do the right thing?

5

☐ Me
☐ My Partner

*W*hich is more important: education or experience?

6

☐ Me
☐ My Partner

*H*ow often do you call your parents?

Huh?

Questions about little, seemingly insignificant facets of your personality may actually shed the most light on who you are.

1

☐ Me
☐ My Partner

*D*o you fold your underwear or just stuff it in the drawer?

2

☐ Me
☐ My Partner

At what age will you let your children date?

3

☐ Me
☐ My Partner

Would you rather go to Mardi Gras in New Orleans, or New Year's Eve in Times Square?

4

☐ Me
☐ My Partner

Would you rather go to the Moon or to Mars?

5

☐ Me
☐ My Partner

What three famous living people would you like to be friends with?

Discover your lover

Yikes!

Do you like a good scare? A good surprise? Do you like roller coasters? Do you like surprise birthday parties?

1
- ❑ Me
- ❑ My Partner

*W*hat's the luckiest thing that's ever happened to you?

2
- ❑ Me
- ❑ My Partner

*W*hat's the weirdest/creepiest/ thing that's ever happened to you?

3
- ❑ Me
- ❑ My Partner

*C*an you sing the theme song to *The Flintstones? The Brady Bunch? The Jetsons? Gilligan's Island? The Partridge Family? The Addams Family?* Your favorite TV show?

4
- ❑ Me
- ❑ My Partner

*W*ho is in charge of the TV remote control in your relationship?

5

☐ Me
☐ My Partner

*W*hat activity do you like to do that's "on the edge"?

If

This isn't just idle dreaming…it's a door to your secret dreams and desires. Will you share them with your partner?

1

☐ Me
☐ My Partner

*I*f you could be any age for a day, what age would you be?

2

☐ Me
☐ My Partner

*I*f you could change one thing about your parents, what would it be? How would you be different now if that change had been made when you were a child?

3

☐ Me
☐ My Partner

If you had one million dollars that you had to give away, who or what would you give it to?

4

☐ Me
☐ My Partner

If you could become invisible for a week, what would you do?

5

☐ Me
☐ My Partner

If you ran Mattel Toy Company, what new toys would you create?

6

☐ Me
☐ My Partner

If you were head of the United Nations, how would you try to promote world peace?

7

☐ Me
☐ My Partner

If you could organize all of your days to suit your personality perfectly, what would each 24 hour period look like?

8

□ Me
□ My Partner

*I*f you could be any height and weight, what would they be?

Kid Stuff

A lot of your behavior today is based on your experiences during the first 10 years of your life. How much do you remember of that time?

1

□ Me
□ My Partner

*W*hat was your favorite toy when you were young?

2

□ Me
□ My Partner

*D*id you ever have a nickname?

3

□ Me
□ My Partner

*D*id you have a favorite pet when you were a kid?

4

❑ Me
❑ My Partner

*W*ho was your Very Best Friend at various ages? What are your best memories of your times together? Where are they now?

5

❑ Me
❑ My Partner

*H*ow many brothers and sisters do you have? Do you think your birth order has affected your personality?

Memories

Do you remember when life was simpler, less complicated?
(Or does it only seem that way?!)

1

❑ Me
❑ My Partner

*D*o you remember your very first kiss?

2
. . .

☐ Me

☐ My Partner

*W*ho was your very first girlfriend or boyfriend?

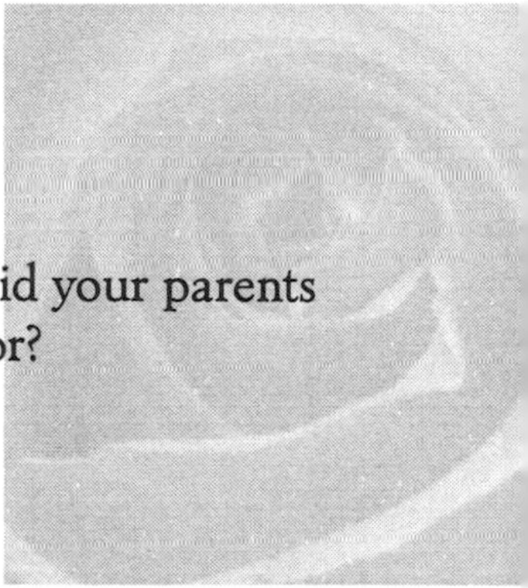

3
. . .

☐ Me

☐ My Partner

*W*hat one thing did your parents always yell at you for?

4
. . .

☐ Me

☐ My Partner

*W*hat did you get away with in high school that you've still never told anyone about?

5
. . .

☐ Me

☐ My Partner

*W*hat is your earliest memory of childhood?

Miscellaneous

Unusual questions challenge your normal ways of thinking;
they challenge your assumptions. They thereby help to
reveal who you really are.

1

☐ Me
☐ My Partner

*Y*ou can create one new national holiday. What is it called, what does it celebrate and what date is it?

2

☐ Me
☐ My Partner

*Y*ou can choose new parents. Who are they?

3

☐ Me
☐ My Partner

*W*hat one part of your body would you change?

4

☐ Me
☐ My Partner

*H*ow many years would you like to live?

5

□ Me   *W*hat would you like your
□ My Partner   epitaph to read?

Miscellaneous, Part II

You'll get the most out of this book by sharing your answers,
your thoughts and your feelings with your partner.

1

□ Me   *W*hat animal would you like
□ My Partner   to be?

2

□ Me   *W*ho would you like to punch in
□ My Partner   the nose?

3

□ Me   *W*hat one bad habit would you
□ My Partner   like to change?

4

☐ Me
☐ My Partner

*W*hat one good habit would you like to start?

5

☐ Me
☐ My Partner

*W*ho's your best friend in all the world?

6

☐ Me
☐ My Partner

*G*od wants an even dozen instead of only Ten Commandments. What are the two new Commandments?

Who Are You?

*Sometimes the simplest, most basic questions
are the most revealing.*

1

☐ Me
☐ My Partner

*H*ow would your best friend describe you?

2
. . .

☐ Me   *H*ow would your worst enemy
☐ My Partner   describe you?

3
. . .

☐ Me   *W*hose ego is more fragile—
☐ My Partner   yours or your partner's?

Who Asked You?

*One would think that answering questions about one's self
would be easy to do. After all, you've lived with yourself
all your life! Curious, isn't it?*

1
. . .

☐ Me   *W*hat book have you been
☐ My Partner   meaning to read?

2
. . .

☐ Me   *W*here in the world have you
☐ My Partner   always wanted to visit?

☐ Me
☐ My Partner

If you were a member of the opposite sex, what would your name be?

Very Interesting

Letting yourself be known—really known—by another person takes time, understanding, patience and trust.

1
. . .

☐ Me
☐ My Partner

Do you tend to have "good luck" or "bad luck"?

2
. . .

☐ Me
☐ My Partner

Are your "hunches" usually right? How often do you act on them?

3
. . .

☐ Me
☐ My Partner

If you were Rick, in the movie *Casablanca*, would you have let Ilsa (Ingrid Bergman) leave at the end?

What!?!

Do you consider yourself to be creative? Is creativity a part of your everyday life? Did you know that the most romantic couples are creatively romantic?

1

☐ Me
☐ My Partner

*W*hen do you feel most creative? During what activities are you most creative?

2

☐ Me
☐ My Partner

*I*f you had just one more day to live, what would you do?

3

☐ Me
☐ My Partner

*I*f you had just six more months to live, what would you do?

Goals

Do you set goals for yourself? Do you write them down?
How do you celebrate when you accomplish them?

1

☐ Me
☐ My Partner

*W*hat five accomplishments are you most proud of?

2

☐ Me
☐ My Partner

*W*hat are your three top goals for this year?

3

☐ Me
☐ My Partner

*W*hat are your top ten goals for your lifetime?

4

☐ Me
☐ My Partner

*I*f you could change one decision you've made in your life, what would it be?

If You Were King

Have you ever said, "What fools! If only I were king (queen) of the world. I'd fix things so they'd work better!" I can't crown you—but I can give you the opportunity to express your opinions:

1
. . .

☐ Me
☐ My Partner

*W*ould the world be better off without money? Taxes? TV? Religion? The opposite sex? The Pill? Computers? Rock music? Rap music? Opera? Football? Cars? Fundamentalists? Conservatives? Liberals? Spiders? *Playboy Magazine*? Atomic weapons? Welfare? Cigarettes? Farm subsidies? Congress? Credit cards? Video games? Handguns? Lawyers? Talk shows? Speed limits? The Internet? Advertising? TV weather reporters? Mandatory schooling? Communism? Capitalism? Socialism? The Academy Awards? Daily newspapers? Fast food? So many cookbooks? Therapists? Advice columnists? The common cold? Drugs? Chocolate?

Money

Studies show that couples fight about money more than any other issue. You don't need to see eye-to-eye, but you'll get along much better if you understand each other's attitudes about money.

1

☐ Me
☐ My Partner

*Y*ou've just been given a million dollars (tax free). What is the first thing you'll do tomorrow morning?

2

☐ Me
☐ My Partner

*Y*ou just found a wallet with $500 cash in it. What will you do with it?

3

☐ Me
☐ My Partner

*Y*ou have $2 million to spend specifically on a collection of some kind. What would you buy?

Money, Part II

What role does money play in your life? Can you think of more creative ways to use money than to simply buy gifts for your partner?

1

☐ Me
☐ My Partner

*I*f you're so smart, why aren't you a millionaire?

2

☐ Me
☐ My Partner

*W*ould you ever spend $300 on a bottle of wine?

3

☐ Me
☐ My Partner

*H*ow much tip do you give in restaurants? To taxi drivers? To hotel attendants? To a waiter who's given you lousy service?

4

☐ Me
☐ My Partner

*S*hould taxes be reduced? Should rich people pay more taxes?

☐ Me
☐ My Partner

*W*hat is your definition of "rich"?

More Money

Do you feel better when you have money in the bank?
Do you feel good about the way you earn money?

1
. . .

☐ Me
☐ My Partner

*A*re you good or bad with money?

2
. . .

☐ Me
☐ My Partner

*A*re you a big spender or a cheap-skate?

3
. . .

☐ Me
☐ My Partner

*S*hould couples have joint or individual bank accounts?

4

☐ Me
☐ My Partner

*H*ow many credit cards do you have? Why?

5

☐ Me
☐ My Partner

*W*hich would be worse: losing your wallet or being embarrassed in public?

6

☐ Me
☐ My Partner

*D*o you believe that love of money is the root of evil?

More or Less

Let's face it, we all compare ourselves with others.
We can't help it...So let's at least be honest about it!

1

☐ Me
☐ My Partner

*A*re you more or less ambitious than your co-workers?

2

❏ Me
❏ My Partner

*A*re you more or less spiritual than your partner?

3

❏ Me
❏ My Partner

*A*re you more or less intelligent than most people?

4

❏ Me
❏ My Partner

*A*re you more or less sensitive than most people?

5

❏ Me
❏ My Partner

*A*re you more or less moral than most people?

6

❏ Me
❏ My Partner

*A*re you more or less sensual than most people?

(More of) More or Less

The goal is not to be "Number One" in every category.
Rather, it's to understand yourself, your talents and
your limitations in relationship to others.

1

☐ Me
☐ My Partner

*A*re you more or less mature
than most people?

2

☐ Me
☐ My Partner

*A*re you more or less thoughtful
than most people?

3

☐ Me
☐ My Partner

*A*re you more or less competitive
than most people?

4

☐ Me
☐ My Partner

*A*re you more or less healthy
than most people?

5

☐ Me
☐ My Partner

*A*re you more or less emotionally stable than most people?

Movie Inspired Questions

Movies have always explored the questions of love.
Do you agree with their conclusions? What do you think of the
movies' portrayal of love? Of men? Of women?

1

☐ Me
☐ My Partner

*C*an men and women be just friends? (*When Harry Met Sally*)

2

☐ Me
☐ My Partner

*W*hat is your quest? (*Monty Python and the Holy Grail*)

3

☐ Me
☐ My Partner

*W*ould you sleep with a stranger for a million dollars? (*Indecent Proposal*)

4

. . .

☐ Me
☐ My Partner

$\mathscr{I}$s there one Perfect Person for everyone? (*Sleepless In Seattle*)

Musical Interludes

Music has been called the "Language of Love."
Do you agree? How do you use music to express your love?

1

. . .

☐ Me
☐ My Partner

$\mathscr{Y}$our favorite singer is writing a song about you. What's the title of the song? Sing it.

2

. . .

☐ Me
☐ My Partner

$\mathscr{W}$hat's your favorite type of music? Favorite singer? Favorite musical group?

3

☐ Me
☐ My Partner

*W*hat's your favorite song? Favorite dance tune? Favorite ballad? Favorite classical piece? Favorite love song?

4

☐ Me
☐ My Partner

*D*id your parents sing you to sleep at night? What songs did they sing?

Nighty-Night

You'll spend a quarter to a third of your life in bed.
So let's make the most of it!

1

☐ Me
☐ My Partner

*A*re you a sound sleeper?

2

☐ Me
☐ My Partner

*D*o you remember your dreams? Do you dream in color?

3
. . .

☐ Me
☐ My Partner

*D*o you have to sleep on the same side of the bed all the time?

4
. . .

☐ Me
☐ My Partner

*W*hat is your favorite position to sleep with your partner: spoons, bookends, pretzels, or something else?

Okay?

Your values are reflected in the kinds of things you approve of and disapprove of. What kinds of issues are you adamant about, and what kinds are you flexible on?

1
. . .

☐ Me
☐ My Partner

*I*s it okay for people of different races to date? To marry? To have children?

2

☐ Me
☐ My Partner

*I*s it okay for your partner to have a best friend—of the opposite sex?

3

☐ Me
☐ My Partner

*I*s it okay to lie under certain circumstances? What's the difference between a "little white lie" and other kinds of lies?

4

☐ Me
☐ My Partner

*I*s it okay to lie to avoid hurting someone's feelings?

One Day at a Time

Personally, I have a hard time grasping the timeframe of a year.
It's such a lot of time! A month is long, too. Weeks are okay...
but a day—one day at a time—is just the right amount of time.
I can deal with that. How about you?

1

☐ Me
☐ My Partner

*W*hat holiday do you most look forward to every year? What holiday or event do you dread the most?

2

☐ Me
☐ My Partner

*W*hat are your most and least favorite days of the week? Why? What could you do to ease the pain?

3

☐ Me
☐ My Partner

*I*f you had one extra hour each day, what would you do with it? If you had one extra day each week, what would you do with it?

People

How many people do you like to be with? Lots, like at a party?
A few, like at an intimate get-together? Just the two of you?
Or do you prefer to be alone?

1

☐ Me
☐ My Partner

*I*f you could have a conversation with one famous person in history, who would it be? What would you talk about?

2

☐ Me
☐ My Partner

*I*f you could talk with a *fictional* person, who would it be?

3

☐ Me
☐ My Partner

*W*ho are the three greatest people in history?

4

☐ Me
☐ My Partner

*D*o you know someone who really needs your advice? What advice would you give him/her?

5

☐ Me
☐ My Partner

$\mathcal{W}$ho are the people for whom you would do *anything?*

Perfect

Nobody's perfect—but the idea of what you consider to be perfect/ultimate/awesome tells us a lot about you.

1

☐ Me
☐ My Partner

$\mathcal{W}$hat's your idea of the Perfect Date?

2

☐ Me
☐ My Partner

$\mathcal{W}$hat would the Perfect Weekend consist of?

3

☐ Me
☐ My Partner

$\mathcal{W}$hat's your idea of the Perfect Kiss?

☐ Me
☐ My Partner

4

$\mathscr{W}$hat would Perfect Sex be like?

☐ Me
☐ My Partner

5

$\mathscr{W}$hat would the Perfect Vacation be like?

Philosophy 101

You may not think of yourself as a "philosopher," but everyone has a "philosophy of life"—a set of beliefs that guide our actions; a view of life that explains why things are the way they are.

☐ Me
☐ My Partner

1

$\mathscr{W}$hy does the world exist?

☐ Me
☐ My Partner

2

$\mathscr{H}$ow did the universe begin?

3
. . .

□ Me
□ My Partner

*W*hat one book should everyone in the world be required to read?

4
. . .

□ Me
□ My Partner

*W*hat is your Philosophy of Life?

5
. . .

□ Me
□ My Partner

*I*s there one phrase that sums up your philosophy?

Power

They say that power corrupts. Do you think you could wield power well and responsibly? How do you handle power in your life right now?

1
. . .

□ Me
□ My Partner

*I*f you were President of the United States of America, what's the first thing you would do?

2

☐ Me
☐ My Partner

If you were the Pope, what would you do?

3

☐ Me
☐ My Partner

Who has more power in our society, men or women? Who has more power in your relationship, you or your partner?

4

☐ Me
☐ My Partner

If you ran the nation's school system, what changes would you make?

Psychological Stuff

Do you know what's going on inside your head? Do you know what's going on inside your lover's head? You might want to look into it!

1

☐ Me
☐ My Partner

What motivates you to do your best?

2

☐ Me
☐ My Partner

*H*ow do you handle uncertainty?

3

☐ Me
☐ My Partner

*W*hat are you afraid of? (Fear of failure? Rejection? Abandonment? Your own anger? Others' anger? Inadequacy?)

4

☐ Me
☐ My Partner

*U*nder what circumstance would you seek the help of a counselor or therapist for yourself? Would you consider seeing a couple's counselor if your partner felt it was necessary?

5

☐ Me
☐ My Partner

*W*hat do you feel is your life's central emotional challenge? Intellectual challenge? Career challenge?

Yin and Yang

The world, our lives and our relationships are in constant flux.
Energy ebbs and flows. We are all different—yet the same.
How do you deal with it all?!

1
. . .

☐ Me
☐ My Partner

*W*hat do you believe is the biggest difference between men and women?

2
. . .

☐ Me
☐ My Partner

*D*o you believe that opposites attract? Do you think that's a good basis for a loving relationship?

3
. . .

☐ Me
☐ My Partner

*D*o you tend to see things as black-and-white, or as shades of grey?

4
. . .

☐ Me
☐ My Partner

*H*ow consistent are your actions with your beliefs? How do you handle your own inconsistencies?

5
. . .

☐ Me

☐ My Partner

*W*hat lessons should be learned from children? From senior citizens?

Romance

Do you have enough romance in your life right now?
How important is romance in your life?

1
. . .

☐ Me

☐ My Partner

*W*hat's the most romantic thing you've ever done?

2
. . .

☐ Me

☐ My Partner

*W*hat's the most romantic thing that's ever been done for you?

3
. . .

☐ Me

☐ My Partner

*H*ave you ever had a broken heart? How long did it take to heal?

4
. . .

☐ Me
☐ My Partner

*H*ow do you define "Romance"?

5
. . .

☐ Me
☐ My Partner

*W*ho's more romantic, men or women? Why do you suppose this is?

Say It

We all keep a lot of things inside: feelings, longings, resentments, desires. Sometimes it's good to express them. Sometimes simply acknowledging them is enough.

1
. . .

☐ Me
☐ My Partner

*W*hat would you like to say to your father, but you just haven't been able to bring yourself to do it?

2
. . .

☐ Me
☐ My Partner

*W*hat would you like to say to your mother? Your brothers or sisters?

3
. . .

☐ Me
☐ My Partner

*W*hat do you wish you could say to your boss, but you don't because you'd probably get fired?

4
. . .

☐ Me
☐ My Partner

*H*ave you ever said anything that you wish you could take back?

School Daze

Did you like school? Were you a member of the "in" crowd?
Did you study much? Did you worry about school?

1
. . .

☐ Me
☐ My Partner

*W*hat was your best subject in Grade School? High School? College?

2

☐ Me
☐ My Partner

*W*hat was your *worst* subject?

3

☐ Me
☐ My Partner

*W*ho was your best teacher? What did he or she teach you?

4

☐ Me
☐ My Partner

*Y*ou can go back and change one thing that happened to you in high school. What would you change—and how would this affect your life today?

5

☐ Me
☐ My Partner

*D*o you remember your first school dance? Your third grade teacher? Your worst experience in gym class?

Science Fiction

*Technology advances, science expands the frontiers of knowledge,
but human nature remains the same: we'll always be struggling
with the mysteries of love.*

1

☐ Me
☐ My Partner

*W*hich would you rather have:
a time machine or a matter
transfer device?

2

☐ Me
☐ My Partner

*W*hich Star Trek series is best?

3

☐ Me
☐ My Partner

*I*f you had access to a holo-deck
(like they have on *Star Trek: The Next
Generation*), how would you use it?

4

☐ Me
☐ My Partner

*W*hich would you rather explore:
outer space, the ocean depths or the
psychic frontier?

Secrets

Skeletons in the closet??—Who me? Not me! No way!
What would make you think such a thing?
[Well, maybe there was this one time...]

1

☐ Me
☐ My Partner

*H*ave you ever told something to a stranger on a plane that you haven't told your partner?

2

☐ Me
☐ My Partner

*H*ave you ever cheated in school? On your taxes?

3

☐ Me
☐ My Partner

*A*re there any family secrets that you carry with you?

Intimate Fantasies

Kids know how to fantasize without being taught.
We adults have to re-learn how to let our imaginations
run wild again.

1

☐ Me
☐ My Partner

*W*hat is your secret sexual fantasy?
(You know, that one that you've
never shared with anyone.)

2

☐ Me
☐ My Partner

*W*here would you like to have sex?

3

☐ Me
☐ My Partner

*I*deally, how often would you like
to have sex?

4

☐ Me
☐ My Partner

*W*hat kind of clothing do you
find sexy?

☐ Me
☐ My Partner

*W*hat kind of lingerie do you prefer?

Foreplay

Here's where we're really going to uncover some assumptions between the two of you. Hang in there!

1

☐ Me
☐ My Partner

*D*o you know what your partner's favorite foreplay activity is?

2

☐ Me
☐ My Partner

*W*hat is your favorite foreplay activity? To give? To receive?

3

☐ Me
☐ My Partner

*C*an you describe an orgasm? (What color is it? Does it tingle, explode, flow? Does it linger? How long? How else would you describe it?)

4

❑ Me
❑ My Partner

*D*o you feel comfortable asking your partner for specific kinds of stimulation?

Sex

As a culture we are obsessed with sex.
And yet we rarely really talk about it.

1

❑ Me
❑ My Partner

*W*ould you rather be rich or sexy?

2

❑ Me
❑ My Partner

*W*ould you like to have sex outside? Would you do it if your partner wanted to?

3

❑ Me
❑ My Partner

*W*ould you ever have sex in an elevator? What outrageous location would excite you?

4

□ Me
□ My Partner

*W*ould you like to join the Mile High Club?

5

□ Me
□ My Partner

*H*ave you ever had sex in your living room? In the laundry room? On the kitchen table?

6

□ Me
□ My Partner

*H*ow has your sexuality changed over the years?

7

□ Me
□ My Partner

*I*f your children are sexually active at the same age that you were, will that be okay with you?

8

□ Me
□ My Partner

*W*hat sexual activity have you never before done and would like to try?

Hot Stuff!

*What are your personal turn-ons? You don't have to tell
all of us—just your very own intimate partner.*

1

☐ Me
☐ My Partner

*H*ave you ever made love in the
back seat of a car?

2

☐ Me
☐ My Partner

*W*hat are your favorite erotic
and/or sexy movies?

3

☐ Me
☐ My Partner

*W*ould you like your lover to be
more sexually assertive? How—
specifically?

4

☐ Me
☐ My Partner

*W*hat songs make you think of
making love? Do you own them?

5
. . .

☐ Me
☐ My Partner

*H*ow did you first learn about sex? What crazy misconceptions did you once have?

Simply Outrageous!

There is a time and a place for acting mature and grown up. But it's not always and everywhere! What is the most wild/outrageous part of your personality?

1
. . .

☐ Me
☐ My Partner

*Y*ou can commit one crime and get away with it completely. What would that crime be?

2
. . .

☐ Me
☐ My Partner

*I*f you could be a super hero, who would you be?

3

❏ Me
❏ My Partner

*I*f you could be a *new* super hero (with new powers), what would you call yourself, and what would your powers be?

4

❏ Me
❏ My Partner

*I*f you were going to get a tattoo...what would it be? And where on your body would it be?

Smarty Pants!

There are many ways of being "smart"—just as there are many ways of being romantic.

1

❏ Me
❏ My Partner

*W*ould you rather be really, really smart, or really, really good looking?

2

☐ Me
☐ My Partner

*H*ow are you smart? What are your best talents?

3

☐ Me
☐ My Partner

*A*re your decisions usually right?

4

☐ Me
☐ My Partner

*I*f you had and I.Q. of 190, how would it change your life?

Stuff

You're surrounded by stuff. Some of it is yours, some of it belongs to others, some of it you share. How do you and your partner deal with your stuff?

1

☐ Me
☐ My Partner

*W*hat's your favorite stuff? (What are your favorite possessions?)

2

- ☐ Me
- ☐ My Partner

*W*hat was your favorite stuff when you were a baby? A child? An adolescent?

3

- ☐ Me
- ☐ My Partner

*W*hat do you carry in your pockets? In your purse? In your briefcase?

4

- ☐ Me
- ☐ My Partner

*W*hat is the single most expensive item you own?

5

- ☐ Me
- ☐ My Partner

*W*hat personal item do you value the most?

Supercalifragilisticexpialidocious

Does everything have to make sense?
How imaginative are you?

1

☐ Me
☐ My Partner

*W*hat are the three greatest inventions of all time?

2

☐ Me
☐ My Partner

*W*ould you rather have the power to become invisible or the power to levitate things?

3

☐ Me
☐ My Partner

*I*f you could have great talent in one area, which would you choose to be: a writer, artist or musician? Why?

Time

Think about it: Time is your most precious resource of all. Do you use it wisely? How much of it do you spend on your relationship?

1

☐ Me
☐ My Partner

If you could save time in a bottle, what would you do with it? (Thank you, Jim Croce.)

2

☐ Me
☐ My Partner

What is your favorite time of day?

3

☐ Me
☐ My Partner

What is your favorite season?

4

☐ Me
☐ My Partner

If there were eight days in a week, what would you do with that extra day?

Discover your lover

☐ Me
☐ My Partner

*H*ow many minutes of undivided attention per day do you give your partner?

Togetherness

It seems to be human nature to want to "couple-up."
Maybe it's true that two heads are better than one!

1

☐ Me
☐ My Partner

*C*an a person be *too much* in love?

2

☐ Me
☐ My Partner

*C*an you read your partner's mind?

3

☐ Me
☐ My Partner

*I*f you could dress your partner, how would you dress him/her?

4

☐ Me
☐ My Partner

*I*s your lover your best friend?

5

☐ Me
☐ My Partner

*W*hat is the best relationship advice you've ever gotten?

Potpourri

Your thoughts, opinions and unique points-of-view make you who you are. Who are you?

1

☐ Me
☐ My Partner

*D*o you have a guardian angel?

2

☐ Me
☐ My Partner

*D*o you have neat handwriting? What does your signature reveal about your personality?

3

☐ Me
☐ My Partner

*A*re you happy with your name?
What would you change it to?

TV

*It's said that the average American watches seven hours of
TV per day! While this certainly doesn't apply to you,
what are your TV habits?*

1

☐ Me
☐ My Partner

A new TV sitcom is going to be
created, based on your life. What is the
name of the show? Describe the major
characters. What is the basic plot?

2

☐ Me
☐ My Partner

*O*prah is going to devote a whole
show to you. Complete this phrase:
"Next, on Oprah, (_____)."

3

☐ Me
☐ My Partner

*W*hat, in your opinion, is the Greatest TV Show In The World? Why?

4

☐ My Partner
☐ My Partner

*W*hat TV show are you embarrassed to admit that you enjoy?

TV, Part II

The Boob Tube; the Great American Invention; the One-Eyed Monster. Has it eaten your brain? Do you spend as much time with your partner as with the TV??

1

☐ Me
☐ My Partner

*H*ow many hours of TV do you watch in an average day?

2

☐ Me
☐ My Partner

*I*s there too much violence on TV? Too much sex?

3

□ Me
□ My Partner

*Y*ou've just been made president of NBC. What changes would you make?

4

□ Me
□ My Partner

*T*he TV show *60 Minutes* is going to do an expose on you. What skeletons have they discovered in your closet? How will you respond?

Your Life

It's your life. You're in charge. You get to make all the decisions. Cool, huh?

1

□ Me
□ My Partner

*T*hey're going to make a movie about your life. What kind of movie is it? (Comedy, tragedy, adventure, science fiction, romance?) What is the title of the movie? Who stars in it? Who plays you?

2

- Me
- My Partner

*B*arbara Walters is going to interview you for TV. What are her first three questions to you?

3

- Me
- My Partner

*W*ho is your mentor? Hero? Role model?

4

- Me
- My Partner

*I*magine that your life is a story—a novel. And you are the author. What is the title of this novel? What chapter are you now living? What kind of story are you going to write (live) over the next ten, twenty, thirty, forty years?

Weird Science

Let your imagination run wild...Where will it lead you?

1

☐ Me
☐ My Partner

*I*f you could change one of the Laws of Physics, which one would it be? What would the new law be?

2

☐ Me
☐ My Partner

*I*f you could live in the past, what year would you go to, and what location would you go to?

3

☐ Me
☐ My Partner

*I*f you could live in the future, what year would you go to, and what location would you go to?

4

☐ Me
☐ My Partner

*I*f you had been the first person on the Moon, what would you have said as you stepped onto the surface?

You!

Let's get personal. These questions tap into some private parts of your personality. Are you willing to share them?

1

☐ Me
☐ My Partner

*W*ould you rather be rich or famous?

2

☐ Me
☐ My Partner

*I*f you could save just one object from your burning home, what would it be?

3

☐ Me
☐ My Partner

*W*hat is your very best quality? (This is not the time to be modest.)

4

☐ Me
☐ My Partner

*W*hat is your very worst quality? What is the dark side of your personality? (How do you deal with it? Ignore it? Fight it? Give in to it? Harness it?)

You, Part II

*You are a fascinating person! There never was another person
exactly like you, and there never will be again!*

1

☐ Me
☐ My Partner

*A*re you open-minded?
(Does your partner agree?)

2

☐ Me
☐ My Partner

*W*hat traditions are important to
you? (Family traditions? Religious
traditions? Holiday traditions?)

3

☐ Me
☐ My Partner

*I*f you had to be either blind or
deaf, which would you choose?

4

☐ Me
☐ My Partner

*W*hat is your most cherished
photo?

□ Me

*W*ho do you need to forgive?

□ My Partner

You Too

This is about you. And about your partner, too.
The two of you. The more you know about each other,
the deeper your love can grow.

1
. . .

□ Me

*W*hat makes you nostalgic?

□ My Partner

Homesick? Thoughtful?

2
. . .

□ Me

*W*hat gives you the creeps?

□ My Partner

3
. . .

□ Me

*W*hat makes you horny?

□ My Partner

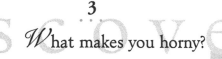

4

❏ Me
❏ My Partner

*W*hat fascinates you?

You Two

Let's bring the focus specifically on the two of you.
After all, this is what all these questions are about, right?!

1

❏ Me
❏ My Partner

*H*ow is your relationship the same
as your parents'? How is it different?

2

❏ Me
❏ My Partner

*I*f your partner had an affair,
could you forgive him or her?

3

❏ Me
❏ My Partner

*W*ere the two of you "made
for each other"?

4

· · ·

☐ Me   *H*ow did you know when the two
☐ My Partner   of you had become a "couple"?

Miscellany

There are many, many facets to your personality.
Worth a lifetime of inquiry.

1

· · ·

☐ Me   *W*hat did you want to be when
☐ My Partner   you grew up?

2

· · ·

☐ Me   *I*f men had babies instead of
☐ My Partner   women, how would the world be
different?

3

☐ Me
☐ My Partner

*R*ight this minute—as you are reading this...How is your health? Are you in love? What emotions are you feeling? Do you wish you were doing something else? Do you feel happy?

Opposites

Opposites attract, right? Sometimes yes, sometimes no.

1

☐ Me
☐ My Partner

*H*ow are you and your partner "opposites"?

2

☐ Me
☐ My Partner

*H*ow are you and your partner exactly the same?

3

☐ Me
☐ My Partner

*W*hat was the biggest fight you've ever had with any member of the opposite sex?

4

☐ Me
☐ My Partner

*W*hen you were growing up, what was your relationship like with your parent of the opposite sex?

5

☐ Me
☐ My Partner

*W*hich of your character traits is the most at odds with general cultural norms?

Generations

Your early years have had a vast impact on who you are today. Family and relatives and close friends all leave their mark on us.

1

☐ Me
☐ My Partner

*W*ho is your favorite relative? Why?

2

☐ Me
☐ My Partner

*W*ho is your least favorite relative? Why?

3

☐ Me
☐ My Partner

*W*hat life lesson did you learn from one of your grandparents?

4

☐ Me
☐ My Partner

*W*hat one wish do you have for your children?

5

☐ Me
☐ My Partner

*W*hat is your philosophy on raising children?

Dream On

Dreams are a mysterious phenomenon of our existence. Every belief about them is just a theory. What do you think?

1

☐ Me
☐ My Partner

*D*o you believe that dreams reveal your inner desires? Are dreams a doorway to your unconscious mind?

2

☐ Me
☐ My Partner

*D*o you believe that dreams can foretell the future?

3

☐ Me
☐ My Partner

*D*o you remember any dreams from your childhood?

Fun, Fun, Fun!

While most of us don't really believe that our purpose on earth is to have fun, it certainly makes being here more worthwhile.

1

☐ Me
☐ My Partner

*W*hat's the most fun you've ever had with your clothes on?

2

☐ Me
☐ My Partner

*W*hat's the most fun you've ever had with your clothes off?

3

☐ Me
☐ My Partner

*W*hen you were a kid, did you play with members of the opposite sex? Did you think boys/girls were "yucky"?

4

☐ Me
☐ My Partner

*A*t what age did you start really being interested in the opposite sex?

5

☐ Me
☐ My Partner

*D*o you play enough now?

Think About It

Here are some things that perhaps you've never thought about.
Lucky you—now you have the opportunity!

1

☐ Me
☐ My Partner

*I*f you went bald, would you wear a toupee?

2

☐ Me
☐ My Partner

*W*ould you ever go to a nude beach?

3

☐ Me
☐ My Partner

*W*hat is your favorite planet?

4
. . .

☐ Me
☐ My Partner

*W*hat is your favorite breed of dog? Cat?

5
. . .

☐ Me
☐ My Partner

*I*f you were going to appear on David Letterman's "Stupid Human Tricks" segment, what would you do??

Grades

We get graded in school, but from that point forward we rarely use an objective grading system to evaluate ourselves. It might help!

1
. . .

☐ Me
☐ My Partner

*W*hat grade would you give your relationship? (Grade yourself like in school, A through F.)

2
. . .

☐ Me
☐ My Partner

*W*hat grade would you give your performance at work?

3

☐ Me   *O*n a scale of 1 to 10, how good
☐ My Partner   a secret-keeper are you?

4

☐ Mc   *O*n a scale of 1 to 10, how skilled?
☐ My Partner   a lover are you?

Favorite Things, Part II

*You don't need to defend any of your choices
or preferences. They simply are.*

1

☐ Me   *W*hat is your favorite song?
☐ My Partner   Love song? Dance tune? Classical
                     composition? Instrumental piece?

2

☐ Me   *W*hat is your favorite musical
☐ My Partner   band?

3

❑ Me
❑ My Partner

*W*hat is your favorite magazine?

4

❑ Me
❑ My Partner

*W*ho is your favorite comedian?

For a free one-year subscription to Greg Godek's *LoveLetter Newsletter* send your name and address to:

LoveLetter
Sourcebooks
P.O. Box 372
Naperville, IL 60566

Would you like to see your name in print in a future book?! If you have a romantic, creative or outrageous story that you would like to share, please send it to:

Love Stories
Sourcebooks
P.O. Box 372
Naperville, IL 60566

Would you be interested in having Greg Godek present a speech or seminar to your group? For more information, please call his office at:

630-961-3900

Other books in this series include:

Romantic Dates: Ways to Woo & Wow the One You Love
ISBN: 1-57071-153-4; $6.95

Romantic Fantasies: & Other Sexy Ways of Expressing Your Love
ISBN: 1-57071-154-2; $6.95

Romantic Mischief: The Playful Side of Love
ISBN: 1-57071-151-8; $6.95

Also by Gregory J.P. Godek

1001 Ways to Be Romantic
5th Anniversary Edition of the Bestselling Classic!
ISBN: 1-883518-05-9; $14.95

1001 More Ways to Be Romantic
ISBN: 0-9629803-2-3; $11.95

To order these books or any other of our many publications, please contact your local bookseller, gift store or call Sourcebooks. Books by Gregory J.P. Godek are available in book and gift stores across North America. Get a copy of our catalog by writing or faxing:

Sourcebooks
P. O. Box 372
Naperville, IL 60566
(630) 961-3900
FAX: (630) 961-2168